Healthy Me

Resting and Sleeping

Ryan Wheatcroft   Katie Woolley

WAYLAND

Published in paperback in Great Britain in 2019 by Wayland

Copyright © Hodder and Stoughton, 2018

Editor: Victoria Brooker
Designer: Anthony Hannant, Little Red Ant

ISBN: 978 1 5263 0562 6

10 9 8 7 6 5 4 3 2

Wayland, an imprint of
Hachette Children's Group
Part of Hodder and Stoughton
Carmelite House
50 Victoria Embankment
London EC4Y 0DZ

An Hachette UK Company
www.hachette.co.uk
www.hachettechildrens.co.uk

Printed and bound in China

MIX
Paper from
responsible sources
FSC® C104740

FSC
www.fsc.org

Contents

Why Do We Need To Sleep And Rest?

Sleep is an important part of every day life. Animals sleep, babies sleep, adults sleep and you need sleep, too. Sleep helps to keep you fit and healthy.

When you are asleep, your body has time to repair and replace damaged cells. Sleep also lets your muscles and brain rest after a busy day.

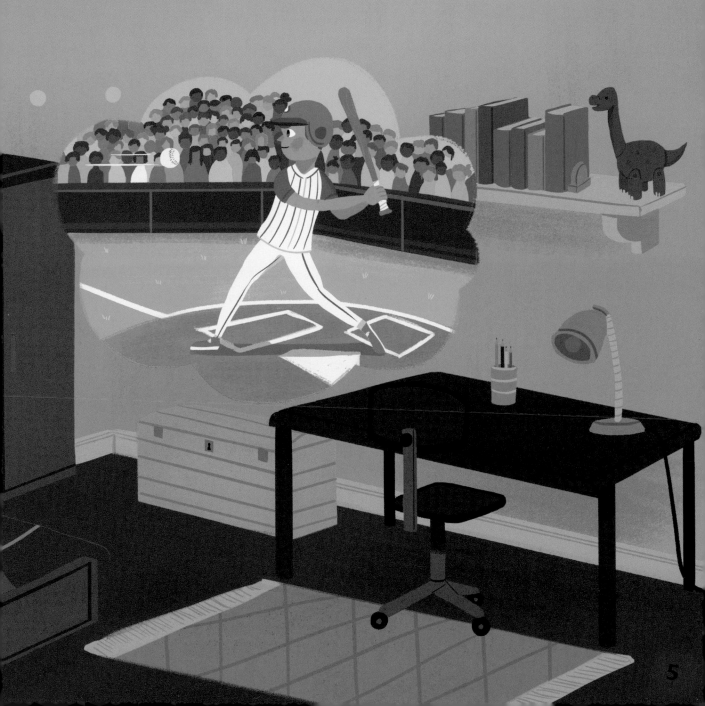

How Much Sleep Do I Need?

Everybody is different as we all have different bodies, so we all need different amounts of sleep! As you get older, you need less sleep.

A newborn baby sleeps for about 17 hours a day.

A one-year-old child sleeps for 13 hours a day.

A four-year-old child needs 11 hours sleep a night.

A seven-year-old child needs 10 hours sleep a night.

Nine and 10 year olds need between 10 and 11 hours sleep a night.

A teenager needs nine hours sleep a night.

Most adults need around eight hours sleep a night.

A Lack of Sleep

When you don't get enough sleep, you start to feel tired and irritable. Exercise and play become hard work and it's more difficult to concentrate at school or enjoy your hobbies.

Scientists think that getting the right amount of sleep also helps you to grow properly. It keeps your immune system healthy and can stop you getting sick.

Day and Night

Your body has a natural clock. Daylight and sunshine help your body realise it's time to wake up and start the day.

As it begins to get dark outside, a hormone called melatonin is released. This makes you feel sleepy and signals that it's time for your body to rest.

Sleep Stages

Every night when you fall asleep, your body passes through five different stages of sleep:

1 Light sleep. This is where your body feels drowsy. You can be woken easily during this stage.

2 True sleep. Your muscles relax, your breathing slows and the speed your heart beats at, called your heart rate, begins to slow down.

3 Deep sleep! Your brain tells your body to lower its blood pressure. This is the force with which your blood pumps around your body. It's quite hard to be woken up during this stage!

4 This is the deepest stage of sleep where it's very difficult to be woken up.

5 REM: This stands for 'rapid eye movement'. During this stage of sleep the brain is very active. This is when you dream!

Drift Off to Dreamland

Everybody dreams but we don't always remember dreaming. If you wake up during REM sleep, you might remember your dream. But, if you wake during other sleep stages you might not.

Dreams are believed to be a way of sorting through the day's events. They help the brain process thoughts and emotions. Your dreams could even give clues as to what you're worrying about.

Take Time to Wind Down

To get a good night's sleep, it can help to exercise during the day. Then, just before bed have a relaxing bath or read your book to wind down.

Try to go to bed at around the same time every night. Your body will get used to this time and you'll fall asleep more quickly. You'll wake up feeling much more alert the next day, too!

Screen Time

Many people spend a lot of time looking at screens, such as computers, televisions, tablets and phones. But did you know that all this 'screen time' could affect your sleep?

A screen's blue light reduces the amount of melatonin your body makes. It becomes harder for you to fall, and stay, asleep. To help you drift off, turn your devices off at least one hour before bedtime.

A Restful Room

A cool, dark and quiet room is ideal when you're trying to fall asleep. Dark curtains will stop your room from being too light. Wearing the right clothes will stop you getting too hot or too cold.

To create a cosy, sleep environment use your room just for sleeping. Don't watch TV, play video games or talk to your friends on the phone when you're in bed. Your body will learn that your bed is the place where you go to sleep.

21

I Just Don't Feel Tired!

Sometimes getting to sleep at night can be hard! You might be excited about a party or worried about a school test the next day. If something is worrying you, talk to an adult you trust.

You could try reading a book to help you relax.
Some people find listening to some music helps, too.
When you start to feel tired, close your eyes and see
if you can fall asleep.

Rest and Relax

It's important to rest each day, too. After lots of exercise and play, or after a long day at school, your brain and body need time to relax.

Reading a book or writing in your diary are good ways to rest. You could do some drawing or play with your toys, too. The important thing is to sit quietly for a bit, rather than rush about.

Yoga Calm

Yoga is one way of being still and quiet for a little while. During a yoga class, your body and mind are relaxed as you focus on the poses and your breathing.

Mindfulness can also help your mental well-being. It's all about paying attention to the present — your feelings and emotions, and to the world around you. This can make you feel less stressed and anxious, helping you to relax and rest.

Top Tips!

Try a yoga class or practise mindfulness to give your mind and body a rest.

Exercise in the day, but not too close to bedtime or you'll feel wide awake!

Turn off electrical devices an hour before bedtime. You'll find you get a better night's rest.

Try to avoid sugary drinks in the afternoon or evening as they can keep you awake.

Keep your room dark, quiet and cool. Ask your parents to help.

29

Teachers' and Parents' Notes

This book is designed for children to begin to learn about the importance of being healthy, and the ways in which we can look after our bodies to keep fit and well. Read the book with children either individually or in groups. Don't forget to talk about the pictures as you go.

Getting a good night's sleep and knowing when to rest are important ways to look after your body. Here are some discussion topics to encourage further thinking about resting and sleeping:

 Why is it so important to get enough sleep every night?

 How do you feel after a bad night's sleep?

 Can you name four things you could do before bedtime to wind down?

 When is it best to exercise, during the day or right before bedtime? Why do you think that is?

Activities you can do:

 Try keeping a 'sleep log' of how much sleep you get over the course of a week. Have you had enough sleep, do you think?

 Try keeping a 'screen time log' of when you use electronic devices, such as computers, televisions, tablets and phones. How much time do you use electronic devices during each day/each week? Do you always turn these off at least an hour before bedtime? Is there any connection between your 'screen time' log and your 'sleep log'?

 Can you remember a dream you've had? Why not try drawing it!

Further reading

Sleep Easy: A Mindfulness Guide to Getting a Good Night's Sleep by Paul Christelis and Elisa Paganelli (Watts, 2018)
Good Night Yoga: A Pose-by-Pose Bedtime Story by Mariam Gates and Sarah Jane Hinder (Sounds True, 2015)

Glossary

cells the basic structures that make up the body
concentrate to focus your attention on one activity
environment your surroundings
hormone a substance in the body, produced by cells, that regulates a
certain activity
immune system the organs and processes of the body that
fight infections
irritable to get easily wound up and annoyed by little things
melatonin a hormone released by the body that regulates sleep
and wakefulness
muscles tissues in the body that contract to produce movement or
keep a part of the body in position

Index